Blessed Leaves

Bahá'í Prayers and Writings for Girls

Bellwood Press
1233 Central St., Evanston, IL 60201

Published 2025
Printed in the United States of America
28 27 26 25 1 2 3 4

ISBN 978-1-61851-270-3

A Note to the Reader

The prayers and passages collected in this book all have one thing in common: the individuals they were addressed to or written for were women and girls. While this makes for a special collection, and one that has been designed and curated with girls in mind, it does not mean that these words are only for girls or women to read.

It is very important to understand that all of the Bahá'í writings are for all people, regardless of who they were addressed to or what pronouns they use.

All prayers are for anyone who wishes to turn their heart toward God.

I am, O my Lord,
Thy handmaiden,
who hath hearkened to Thy call,
and hastened unto Thee,
fleeing from herself
and resting her heart upon Thee.
I implore Thee, O my Lord,
by Thy name out of which
all the treasures of the earth
were brought forth,
to shield me from the hints
of such as have disbelieved in Thee
and repudiated Thy truth.
Powerful art Thou to do
what Thou pleasest.
Thou art, verily,
the All-Knowing, the All-Wise.

Bahá'u'lláh

Cleanse me
with the waters of Thy mercy,
O my Lord,
and make me wholly Thine,
and cause me to approach
the Tabernacle of Thy Cause
and the adored Sanctuary
of Thy Presence.
Ordain, then, for me
all the things
Thou didst ordain
for the chosen ones among
Thy handmaidens,
and rain down upon me
that which will illuminate
my face and enlighten my heart.
Thou hast power to do
what Thou willest,
and Thou ordainest
what Thou pleasest.

Bahá'u'lláh

We beseech God
to aid all the leaves
to attain the knowledge
of the Tree
and deprive them not
of the ocean of His generosity.
In this day no regard is paid
to loftiness or lowliness,
to poverty or wealth,
to nobility and lineage,
to weakness or might.
Whosoever recognizeth
the incomparable Beloved
is the possessor
of true wealth
and occupieth
a divine station.

Bahá'u'lláh

One of Thy handmaidens,
O my Lord,
hath sought Thy face,
and soared in the atmosphere
of Thy pleasure.
Withhold not from her,
O my Lord,
the things Thou didst ordain
for the chosen ones
among Thy handmaidens.
Enable her, then,
to be so attracted
by Thine utterances
that she will celebrate
Thy praise amongst them.
Potent art Thou
to do what pleaseth Thee.
No God is there but Thee,
the Almighty,
Whose help is implored
by all men.

Bahá'u'lláh

I am one of Thy handmaidens,
O my Lord!
I have turned my face
towards the sanctuary
of Thy gracious favors
and the adored tabernacle
of Thy glory.
Purify me
of all that is not of Thee,
and strengthen me to love Thee
and to fulfill Thy pleasure,
that I may delight myself
in the contemplation of Thy beauty,
and be rid of all attachment
to any of Thy creatures,
and may, at every moment,
proclaim:
“Magnified be God,
the Lord of the worlds!”

Bahá’u’lláh

Withhold not from me,
O my Lord,
the things Thou didst ordain
for such of Thy handmaidens
as circle around Thee,
and on whom
are poured continually
the splendors of the sun
of Thy beauty and the beams
of the brightness of Thy face.
Thou art He
Who from everlasting
hath succored
whosoever hath sought Thee,
and bountifully favored him
who hath asked Thee.
No God is there beside Thee,
the Mighty, the Ever-Abiding,
the All-Bounteous,
the Most Generous.

Bahá'u'lláh

Magnified be Thy name,
O Lord my God!
Behold Thou mine eye
expectant to gaze
on the wonders of Thy mercy,
and mine ear longing to hearken
unto Thy sweet melodies,
and my heart yearning
for the living waters
of Thy knowledge.
Thou seest Thy handmaiden,
O my God,
standing before the habitation
of Thy mercy,
and calling upon Thee
by Thy name
which Thou hast chosen
above all other names
and set up over all that are
in heaven and on earth.

Send down upon her
the breaths of Thy mercy,
that she may be carried
away wholly from herself,
and be drawn entirely
towards the seat which,
resplendent
with the glory of Thy face,
sheddeth afar the radiance
of Thy sovereignty,
and is established
as Thy throne.
Potent art Thou to do
what Thou willest.
No God is there beside Thee,
the All-Glorious,
the Most Bountiful.

Bahá'u'lláh

I am one of Thy handmaidens,
O my Lord!
I have turned my face
towards the habitation
of Thy mercy,
and have sought the wonders
of Thy manifold favors,
inasmuch as all the members
of my body proclaim Thee
to be the All-Bounteous,
He Whose grace is immense.

O Thou Whose face
is the object of my adoration,
Whose beauty is my sanctuary,
Whose court is my goal,
Whose remembrance is my wish,
Whose affection is my solace,
Whose love is my begetter,
Whose praise is my companion,
Whose nearness is my hope,
Whose presence
is my greatest longing
and supreme aspiration!

Disappoint me not,
I entreat Thee,
by withholding
from me the things
Thou didst ordain
for the chosen ones
among Thy handmaidens,
and supply me with the good
of this world
and of the world to come.
Thou art, verily,
the Lord of creation.
No God is there beside Thee,
the Ever-Forgiving,
the Most Bountiful.

Bahá'u'lláh

O thou
handmaid of God!
In this day,
to thank God
for His bounties
consisteth in possessing
a radiant heart,
and a soul open
to the promptings
of the spirit.
This is the essence
of thanksgiving.

'Abdu'l-Bahá

O handmaid of God,
peace must first
be established
among individuals,
until it leadeth in the end
to peace among nations.
Wherefore, O ye Bahá'ís,
strive ye with all
your might to create,
through the power
of the Word of God,
genuine love,
spiritual communion
and durable bonds
among individuals.

'Abdu'l-Bahá

O thou
dear handmaid of God!
If only thou couldst know
what a high station is destined
for those souls
who are severed from the world,
are powerfully
attracted to the Faith,
and are teaching,
under the sheltering shadow
of Bahá'u'lláh!
How thou wouldst rejoice,
how thou wouldst,
in exultation and rapture,
spread thy wings
and soar heavenward . . .

'Abdu'l-Bahá

O Lord!
Help this daughter
of the Kingdom
to be exalted in both worlds;
cause her to turn away
from this mortal world of dust
and from those
who have set
their hearts thereon
and enable her
to have communion
and close association
with the world of immortality.
Give her heavenly power
and strengthen her
through the breaths
of the Holy Spirit
that she may arise
to serve Thee.
Thou art the Mighty One.

ʻAbdu'l-Bahá

O Thou
most glorious Lord!
Make this
little maidservant of Thine
blessed and happy;
cause her to be cherished
at the threshold
of Thy oneness,
and let her drink deep
from the cup of Thy love
so that she may be filled
with rapture and ecstasy
and diffuse
sweet-scented fragrance.
Thou art the Mighty
and the Powerful,
and Thou art
the All-Knowing,
the All-Seeing.

'Abdu'l-Bahá

O thou who hast
bowed thyself down in prayer
before the Kingdom of God!
Blessed art thou,
for the beauty
of the divine Countenance
hath enraptured thy heart,
and the light of inner wisdom
hath filled it full,
and within it shineth
the brightness of the Kingdom.
Know thou that God
is with thee under all conditions,
and that He guardeth thee
from the changes and chances
of this world
and hath made thee
a handmaid
in His mighty vineyard.

'Abdu'l-Bahá

O my Lord,
my Beloved,
my Desire!
Befriend me
in my loneliness
and accompany
me in my exile.
Remove my sorrow.
Cause me to be devoted
to Thy beauty.
Withdraw me
from all else save Thee.

Attract me through
Thy fragrances of holiness.
Cause me to be associated
in Thy Kingdom with those
who are severed
from all else save Thee,
who long to serve
Thy sacred threshold
and who stand to work
in Thy Cause.
Enable me to be one
of Thy maidservants
who have attained
to Thy good pleasure.
Verily,
Thou art the Gracious,
the Generous.

'Abdu'l-Bahá

O Thou kind lord!
Bestow heavenly confirmation
upon this daughter
of the Kingdom
and graciously aid her
that she may remain firm
and steadfast in Thy Cause
and that she may,
even as a nightingale
of the rose-garden of mysteries,
warble melodies
in the Abhá Kingdom
in most wondrous tones,
thereby bringing happiness
to everyone.

Make her exalted
among the daughters
of the Kingdom
and enable her
to attain life eternal.
Thou art the Bestower,
the All-Loving.

'Abdu'l-Bahá

O thou
little handmaid of God!
I earnestly hope
that thou wilt be nurtured
in the bosom
of the love of God
and wilt grow
and develop through
the vitalizing breeze
which wafteth
from the meads
of the Kingdom of heaven,
that thou mayest
become a flourishing tree
beside the stream
of divine knowledge,
laden with fruit
and blossoms and appear
in the utmost freshness
and tender beauty
through the sprinkling
of the clouds of His bounty.

Be assured
that the eye
of His loving-kindness
is directed towards thee
and the glance
of His mercifulness
resteth upon thee.

'Abdu'l-Bahá

References

Page 1: Bahá'u'lláh, *Bahá'í Prayers,* Bahá'í Publishing Trust, 2002, p. 238.

Page 2: Bahá'u'lláh, *Prayers and Meditations,* Bahá'í Publishing Trust, 2014, no. 82.3–4.

Page 5: Bahá'u'lláh, quoted in *Women: Compiled by the Research Department of the Universal House of Justice,* July 1990, no. 6.

Page 6: Bahá'u'lláh, *Bahá'í Prayers,* Bahá'í Publishing Trust, 2002, p. 243.

Page 9: Ibid., pp. 240–41.

Page 10: Ibid., p. 236.

Pages 13–14: Ibid., p. 239.

Pages 17–19: Bahá'u'lláh, *Prayers and Meditations,* Bahá'í Publishing Trust, 2014, no. 98.3–5.

Page 20: 'Abdu'l-Bahá, *Selections from the Writings of 'Abdu'l-Bahá,* Bahá'í Publishing, 2010, no. 153.1.

Page 23: Ibid., no. 201.2.

Page 24: Ibid., no. 64.2.

Page 27: 'Abdu'l-Bahá, *Pearls of Bounty*, Bahá'í Publishing, 2021, p. 8.

Page 28: 'Abdu'l-Bahá, *Bahá'í Prayers and Tablets for Children: A Compilation Prepared by the Research Department of the Universal House of Justice*, 2021, no. 26.

Page 31: 'Abdu'l-Bahá, *Selections from the Writings of 'Abdu'l-Bahá*, Bahá'í Publishing, 2010, no. 91.1.

Page 33–34: 'Abdu'l-Bahá, *Bahá'í Prayers*, Bahá'í Publishing Trust, 2002, pp. 248–49.

Page 36–37: 'Abdu'l-Bahá, *Bahá'í Prayers and Tablets for Children: A Compilation Prepared by the Research Department of the Universal House of Justice*, 2021, no. 26.

Page 39–40: Ibid., no. 29.